I0605952
The World's Best
Christmas
COOKIES
A Sweet Collection of Recipes, Tips & Decorating Ideas, and Inspiration for the Season
BARBOUR
PUBLISHING

Writing and compilation by Nanette Anderson in association with Snapdragon Group℠, Tulsa, OK, USA.

Print ISBN 979-8-89151-162-0

Published by Barbour Publishing, Inc., 1810 Barbour Drive, Uhrichsville, Ohio 44683, www.barbourbooks.com

Our mission is to inspire the world with the life-changing message of the Bible.

Printed in China.

Especially for
From
Date

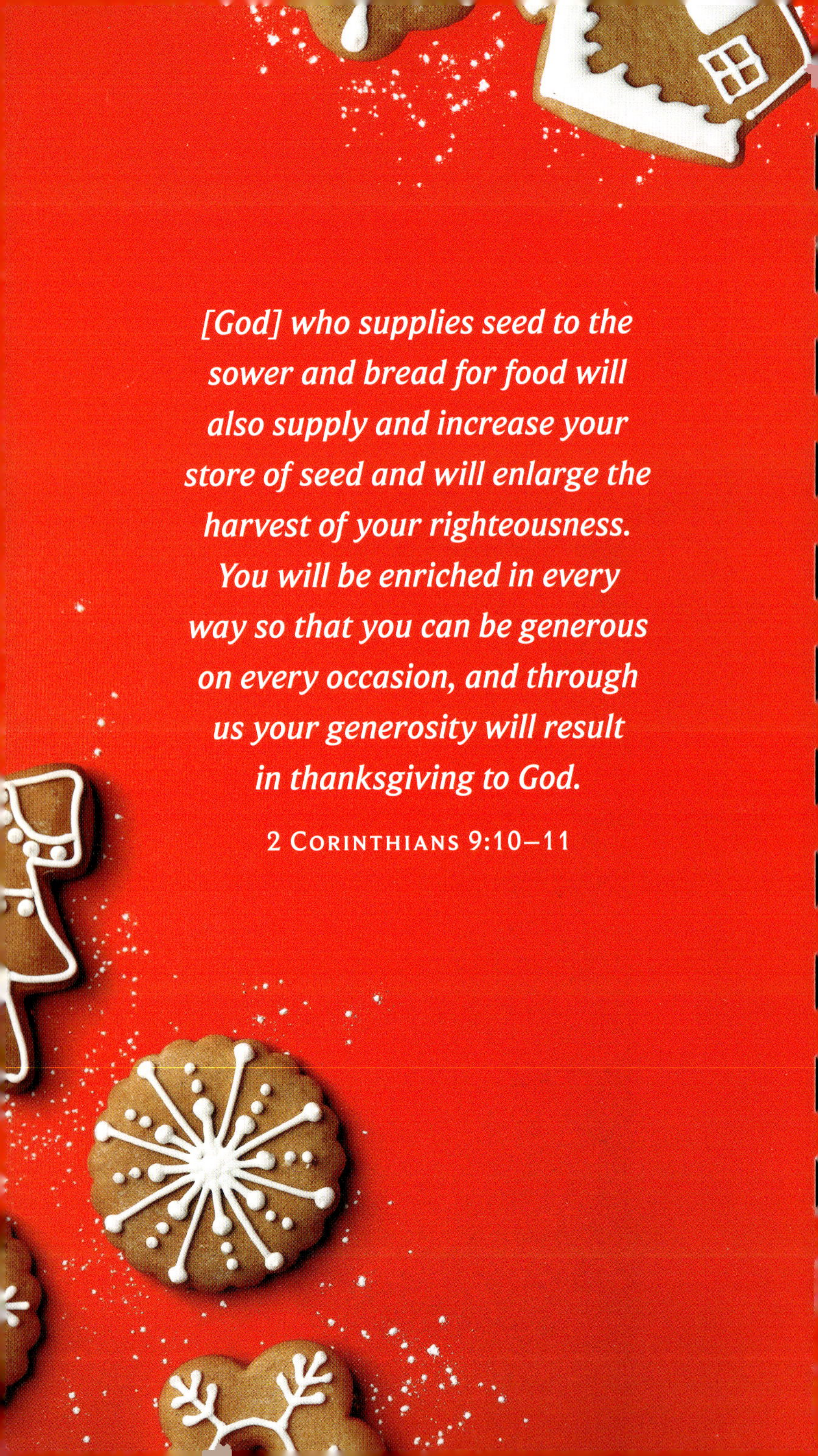

[God] who supplies seed to the sower and bread for food will also supply and increase your store of seed and will enlarge the harvest of your righteousness. You will be enriched in every way so that you can be generous on every occasion, and through us your generosity will result in thanksgiving to God.

2 Corinthians 9:10–11

Contents

Introduction

Birthdays are all about cakes, and Christmas is all about cookies. During the holidays, we pull out our favorite recipes, the ones with the crinkled edges and grease spots, the ones our mothers and grandmothers cherished before us, and the new ones we've been waiting all year to try. We bake like our lives depend on it, enough to eat and plenty to share. It's all part of the wonder of the Christmas season.

The World's Best Christmas Cookies cookbook will bring even more joy to your cookie baking tradition. Before you get out your cookie cutters, find all your trusty cookie sheets, and head out to the store with your list of ingredients, we hope you will take a few minutes to flip through this collection of time-tested recipes. They come with baking tips, family stories, and best wishes from bakers around the country who have agreed to share their family favorites with you.

Consider this collection an early Christmas gift from us to you, one that is certain to add even more delight to your holiday festivities.

Drop Cookies

This type of cookie generally takes the form of a soft dough that can be dropped by spoonfuls or soft balls onto a cookie sheet for baking. It is also the easiest, because no rolling, cutting, or hours of refrigeration are needed. Variety is nearly endless. So if you're needing a quick, easy cookie that beats those pasty, ready-to-bake supermarket varieties, choose one of the great treats in this section!

Coconut Dainties

2 egg whites
¼ teaspoon salt
½ teaspoon vanilla
⅔ cup granulated sugar
1⅓ cups flaked coconut

Beat egg whites, salt, and vanilla until soft peaks form. Add sugar a little at a time, beating until stiff. Fold in coconut and drop by rounded teaspoonfuls onto lightly greased cookie sheet. Bake at 325 degrees for about 20 minutes.

Yield: 1½ dozen

Sweet Tip:

For even baking, keep dropped cookie dough consistent in size.

Christmas Candy Cookies

1 cup shortening
½ cup white sugar
1 cup brown sugar
2 eggs
2 teaspoons vanilla
2¼ cups flour
1 teaspoon baking soda
¾ teaspoon salt
2 cups red and green candy-coated chocolate pieces

Cream together shortening, sugars, eggs, and vanilla. Combine dry ingredients and stir into wet ingredients. Add chocolate candies. Mix and bake at 350 degrees for 10 to 12 minutes.

YIELD: ABOUT 3 DOZEN

Pumpkin Cookies

- 1 cup brown sugar
- 1 cup canned or cooked pumpkin
- ½ cup vegetable oil
- 1 teaspoon vanilla
- 2 cups flour
- 1 teaspoon baking soda
- 1 teaspoon baking powder
- ½ teaspoon salt
- ½ teaspoon cinnamon
- ¼ teaspoon ginger
- ½ teaspoon nutmeg
- 1 cup raisins
- 1 cup walnuts, chopped

Blend together sugar, pumpkin, oil, and vanilla. Combine dry ingredients and stir into wet ingredients, mixing well. Fold in raisins and nuts. Drop by tablespoons onto greased cookie sheet. Bake at 350 degrees for 12 to 15 minutes.

YIELD: 3 TO 4 DOZEN

Christmas Stocking Cookies

5 cups blended oatmeal
2 cups butter
2 cups sugar
2 cups brown sugar
4 eggs
2 teaspoons vanilla
4 cups flour
1 teaspoon salt
2 teaspoons baking powder
2 teaspoons baking soda
24 ounces chocolate chips
1 (8 ounce) milk chocolate bar, grated
3 cups chopped nuts

Measure oatmeal and use a blender to reduce it to fine powder. Cream butter and sugars. Add eggs and vanilla; mix together with flour, oatmeal, salt, baking powder, and baking soda. Add chocolate chips, chocolate bar, and nuts. Drop balls of dough onto lightly greased cookie sheet and bake at 375 degrees for 10 minutes.

YIELD: 2 TO 3 DOZEN

Sweet Tip:

When baking one sheet of cookies at a time, always use the center rack. For dual sheets, reverse them on the racks halfway through their baking time.

Ginger Creams

- ¾ cup shortening
- 1 cup sugar
- 1 egg
- 4 tablespoons molasses
- 2 cups flour
- 2 teaspoons baking soda
- 1 teaspoon cloves
- 1 teaspoon ginger
- 1 teaspoon cinnamon
- Granulated sugar

Mix first nine ingredients well and form into walnut-sized balls. Roll in granulated sugar and bake on greased cookie sheet. Don't flatten the balls. Bake at 350 degrees for 8 to 10 minutes.

YIELD: 2 TO 3 DOZEN

Mrs. Santa's Cinnamon Cookies

½ cup butter
½ cup shortening
1 egg yolk
1 tablespoon light corn syrup
1¼ teaspoons baking soda
2 cups flour
1 tablespoon cinnamon
Sugar

Cream together first four ingredients. Add combined dry ingredients. Mix and chill about an hour. Form into balls and press with fork dipped in sugar. Bake at 375 degrees for 10 to 12 minutes. Let cookies set up for 5 minutes after removing from oven.

YIELD: 2 DOZEN

Sweet Tip:

Even seasoned bakers will forget a crucial step now and then. Unless you are extremely familiar with a recipe, read the instructions through from top to bottom before you begin.

Holiday Fruit Drops

1 cup shortening
2 cups brown sugar
2 eggs
1 teaspoon lemon juice (optional)
½ cup sour milk
3½ cups flour
1 teaspoon baking soda
1 teaspoon salt
2 cups candied cherries, halved or chopped
2 cups chopped dates
1½ cups pecan halves, divided

Mix shortening, sugar, and eggs. Add lemon juice to milk to sour it, if necessary. Stir in soured milk. Blend in combined dry ingredients, cherries, dates, and half the pecans. Chill for 1 hour. Drop by rounded spoonfuls onto lightly greased cookie sheet. Place a pecan half on each cookie and bake at 400 degrees for 8 to 10 minutes. (These cookies actually *improve* with storage.)

YIELD: 2 DOZEN

Oma's Orange Drop Cookies

½ cup shortening
¾ cup sugar
1 egg
½ cup orange juice
2 tablespoons grated orange rind
2 cups flour
½ teaspoon baking powder
½ teaspoon baking soda
½ teaspoon salt

Frosting

1½ cups powdered sugar
2 teaspoons orange rind
1 tablespoon orange juice
3 tablespoons soft butter

Mix together shortening, sugar, and egg. Stir in orange juice and rind. Blend in flour, baking powder, soda, and salt. Drop by spoonfuls onto ungreased cookie sheet and bake at 400 degrees for 8 to 10 minutes. To make frosting, blend powdered sugar, orange rind, orange juice, and butter.

Yield: 2 to 3 dozen

Pecan Care Bears

2 cups flour
¼ cup sugar
½ teaspoon salt
1 cup butter
2 teaspoons vanilla
2½ cups pecans
Powdered sugar

Mix all ingredients except powdered sugar. Form dough into 2-inch balls. Bake on ungreased cookie sheet at 325 degrees for about 15 minutes. Cool slightly and roll in powdered sugar.

YIELD: 3 DOZEN

My husband renamed this popular cookie after our daughter-in-law, Carrie. She makes them every Christmas at our house, and the holidays don't officially begin until there's a batch of Care Bears cooling on the counter!

Coconut Drops

¼ cup butter or margarine
½ cup sugar
1 egg
½ cup milk
½ teaspoon vanilla
½ teaspoon lemon extract
1½ cups flour
1 teaspoon baking powder
½ teaspoon salt
½ cup flaked coconut
Coconut
Maraschino cherries

Cream together butter and sugar. Add egg and beat well; add milk, vanilla, and lemon. Add combined dry ingredients and then add ½ cup coconut. Drop by teaspoons onto greased cookie sheet. Sprinkle a little coconut on each cookie and top with a maraschino cherry. Bake at 375 degrees for about 10 minutes.

YIELD: 2 DOZEN

Applesauce Spice Cookies

1 cup sugar
½ cup shortening
1 egg
1 teaspoon baking soda
1 cup unsweetened applesauce
½ teaspoon salt
2 cups flour
1 teaspoon cinnamon
½ teaspoon cloves
¼ teaspoon nutmeg
1 cup raisins, chopped
1 cup nuts

Cream together sugar, shortening, and egg. Mix baking soda into applesauce and add to creamed mixture. Combine dry ingredients and mix well. Blend in raisins and nuts. Drop onto greased cookie sheet and bake at 350 degrees for 10 to 12 minutes.

YIELD: 2 DOZEN

Snickerdoodles

- ¾ cup sugar
- ½ cup butter or shortening
- 1 egg
- 1¼ cups flour
- ¼ teaspoon salt
- ½ teaspoon baking soda
- 1 teaspoon cream of tartar
- 1 tablespoon sugar
- 1 tablespoon cinnamon

Cream together sugar, butter, and egg. Add flour, salt, baking soda, and cream of tartar. Cover and refrigerate 1 hour. Roll dough into 1-inch balls and dip into sugar/cinnamon mixture. Bake on ungreased cookie sheet at 400 degrees for 10 to 12 minutes.

YIELD: 2 DOZEN

Honey Drops

2½ cups flour
2 cups wheat germ
3 teaspoons baking powder
¼ teaspoon salt
2 eggs
½ cup vegetable oil
1¼ cups honey
½ cup milk
2 teaspoons vanilla
1 teaspoon almond extract

Mix flour, wheat germ, baking powder, and salt and set aside. Blend together eggs and oil. Add honey, milk, and flavoring and mix well. Add dry ingredients until well mixed. Drop by spoonfuls onto parchment-covered cookie sheet and bake at 350 degrees for 10 minutes or until very light brown.

YIELD: 3 TO 4 DOZEN

Old-Fashioned Molasses Cookies

3 cups flour
2 teaspoons baking soda
1 teaspoon salt
1 teaspoon ginger
1 teaspoon cinnamon
¾ cup evaporated milk
¾ tablespoon cider vinegar
1 cup shortening
1 cup sugar
1 egg
½ cup molasses

Stir together flour, baking soda, salt, and spices. Combine evaporated milk and vinegar. Cream shortening and sugar thoroughly and add egg and molasses to it. Beat well. Add milk and vinegar mixture alternately with dry ingredients. Mix well. Drop by spoonfuls onto greased cookie sheet. Bake at 375 degrees for about 10 minutes. Be careful not to overbake.

YIELD: 3 TO 4 DOZEN

Almond Toffee Cookies

4½ cups flour
1 teaspoon baking soda
1 teaspoon cream of tartar
1 teaspoon salt
2 sticks salted butter, softened
1 cup vegetable oil
1 cup powdered sugar
1 cup sugar
2 eggs
1 teaspoon almond extract
1 (10 ounce) package English toffee bits
2 cups sliced almonds, toasted

Whisk together flour, baking soda, cream of tartar, and salt. Cream butter, oil, sugars, eggs, and extract. Combine gradually with flour mixture. Stir in toffee and almonds. Drop by spoonfuls onto ungreased cookie sheet. Bake at 350 degrees for 10 to 12 minutes. Remove from cookie sheet immediately to avoid sticking.

Yield: 4 dozen

Turtle Cookies

2½ cups pecan halves
½ cup water
¾ cup softened butter
½ teaspoon salt
½ cup sugar
1 teaspoon vanilla
1 egg
1½ cups flour
¼ cup cocoa
48 round milk chocolate–covered soft caramels

Soak pecan halves in water while making dough. Drain well. Beat butter, salt, sugar, vanilla, and egg until light and fluffy. Beat in flour and cocoa until dough firms. Place 5 pecan halves in turtle pattern for each cookie on ungreased cookie sheet. Shape dough into 1-inch balls. Place ball on top of each group of 5 pecans, pressing lightly. Bake at 375 degrees for 7 to 10 minutes. Immediately after removing from oven, press 1 caramel gently on top of each cookie. Let cookies set for 3 minutes before removing from sheet.

YIELD: 4 DOZEN

Peanut Butter Cup Cookies

- 1 cup butter, softened
- 1 cup peanut butter
- 1 cup sugar
- 1 cup brown sugar
- 2 eggs
- 2 teaspoons vanilla
- 3½ cups flour
- 2 teaspoons baking soda
- 1 teaspoon salt
- 1 (16 ounce) package miniature peanut butter cups

Blend butter, peanut butter, and sugars until creamy. Add eggs and vanilla and mix well. Combine flour, baking soda, and salt and add to creamed mixture. Shape dough into balls that fit nicely into ungreased miniature muffin tins. Bake at 350 degrees for 5 to 7 minutes. Don't overbake. After removing from oven, immediately press one mini–peanut butter cup into center of each cookie. Let cool in muffin tin.

YIELD: 3 DOZEN

French Lace

1 cup flour
1 cup finely chopped walnuts
½ cup light corn syrup
½ cup shortening
⅔ cup brown sugar

Blend flour and nuts. Bring corn syrup, shortening, and sugar to a boil over medium heat, stirring constantly. Remove from heat and gradually add flour/nut mixture. Drop batter by teaspoonfuls onto lightly greased cookie sheet. Bake only a few cookies at a time at 375 degrees for 5 or 6 minutes. Allow cookies to stand for 5 minutes before removing from baking sheet.

YIELD: 1 TO 2 DOZEN

Carrot Cake Cookies

½ cup melted butter
½ cup brown sugar
¼ cup sugar
1 egg
1½ cups flour
1 teaspoon ground ginger
½ teaspoon salt
1 generous cup carrots, peeled and finely grated
⅓ cup raisins or currants

FROSTING
2 ounces cream cheese, softened
2 ounces butter
¼ cup powdered sugar
½ teaspoon fresh lemon juice

Cream together butter, sugars, and egg. Combine flour, ginger, and salt and blend into creamed mixture. Mix in carrots and raisins/currants. Drop by spoonfuls onto greased cookie sheet and flatten lightly. Bake at 350 degrees for about 10 minutes. Cool. Cream together frosting ingredients and frost.

YIELD: 2 DOZEN

Caramel Apple Cookies

½ cup shortening
1⅓ cups brown sugar
1 egg
2¼ cups flour
1 teaspoon baking soda
½ teaspoon salt
1 teaspoon cinnamon
½ teaspoon cloves
½ teaspoon nutmeg
1 cup grated apple
1 cup raisins
½ cup apple juice
1 cup chopped walnuts

Cream shortening, sugar, and egg. Combine flour, soda, salt, and spices. Add to creamed mixture. Blend in apple, raisins, juice, and nuts. Drop by spoonfuls onto lightly greased baking sheet and bake at 350 degrees for 10 to 12 minutes.

YIELD: 2 TO 3 DOZEN

Spritz Cookies

1 cup margarine
⅔ cup sugar
3 egg yolks
1 teaspoon vanilla
½ teaspoon butter flavoring
2½ cups flour

Mix all ingredients together just until dough forms. Then force dough through cookie press onto ungreased cookie sheet. Bake at 400 degrees for 7 to 10 minutes until set but not brown.

YIELD: 2 DOZEN

Grandma's Raisin Cookies

1 cup raisins
Water
¾ cup shortening
1½ cups sugar
2 eggs
½ cup buttermilk or soured milk
1 teaspoon lemon juice (optional)
3 cups flour
1 teaspoon baking soda
½ teaspoon salt
1 teaspoon cinnamon
1 teaspoon vanilla

Boil raisins gently in water for 5 minutes, and save liquid. Cream shortening, sugar, and eggs. May add lemon juice to milk to sour it. Add milk alternately with combined dry ingredients. Stir in raisins, ½ cup of the saved raisin juice, and vanilla. Drop by spoonfuls onto lightly greased cookie sheet and bake at 350 degrees for about 15 minutes.

YIELD: 3 DOZEN

Chocolate Drops

½ cup shortening
1 cup sugar
1 egg
¾ cup buttermilk
1 teaspoon vanilla
½ cup cocoa
1¾ cups flour
½ teaspoon baking soda
½ teaspoon salt
1 cup chopped nuts

Mix shortening, sugar, and egg. Stir in buttermilk and vanilla. Combine cocoa, flour, soda, and salt. Stir into creamed mixture. Add nuts. Chill for an hour. Drop by spoonfuls onto lightly greased cookie sheet. Bake at 400 degrees for 8 to 10 minutes. Frost with Buttercream Frosting (page 148).

Yield: 2 to 3 dozen

Pineapple Creams

- 1 cup brown sugar
- 1 cup white sugar
- ½ cup butter
- ½ cup shortening
- 2 beaten eggs
- 1 cup crushed pineapple, with juice
- 1 teaspoon vanilla
- 2 teaspoons baking powder
- ½ teaspoon salt
- 1 teaspoon baking soda
- 4 cups flour

Cream sugars, butter, shortening, and eggs. Fold in pineapple and vanilla. Combine dry ingredients and mix well with creamed mixture. Drop by spoonfuls onto greased cookie sheet and bake at 350 degrees for 10 to 12 minutes.

YIELD: 3 DOZEN

Chocolate Mint Snow-Top Cookies

1 (10 ounce) package
  mint-flavored morsels

½ stick softened butter

1 cup sugar

2 eggs

1½ teaspoons vanilla

1½ cups flour

1½ teaspoons baking powder

¼ teaspoon salt

Powdered sugar

Microwave morsels in bowl on high for 1 minute. Stir and let stand while you cream butter, sugar, and eggs. Add melted mints and vanilla. Combine dry ingredients, except powdered sugar, and add to creamed mixture. Wrap in plastic wrap and refrigerate until firm. Shape dough into 1-inch balls, then coat with powdered sugar. Bake on ungreased cookie sheet at 350 degrees for 10 to 12 minutes or until tops appear cracked. Cool on cookie sheet.

YIELD: 2 DOZEN

Pecan Tassies

2 (3 ounce) packages cream cheese, softened
1 cup butter
2 cups flour
½ teaspoon salt

Filling
2 eggs
1½ cups brown sugar
2 tablespoons butter
2 teaspoons vanilla
1½ cups coarsely chopped pecans

Blend cream cheese and butter. Stir in flour and salt and chill 1 hour. Press into ungreased miniature muffin tins and set aside. Beat together eggs, brown sugar, butter, and vanilla. Add nuts and stir. Pour filling over dough in muffin tins. Bake at 325 degrees for about 20 minutes.

Yield: about 4 dozen

Chewy Coconut Macaroons

1 (15 ounce) can
condensed milk

3 cups shredded coconut

Mix together and drop by spoonfuls onto greased cookie sheet. Bake at 350 degrees for about 15 minutes.

Yield: 4 dozen

Sweet Tip:

Cookies will bake much more evenly if you cool the baking sheets after each batch comes out of the oven.

French Macaroons

1 cup blanched almonds
1 cup granulated sugar
2 egg whites, beaten lightly
½ teaspoon vanilla extract
2 tablespoons powdered sugar

Line baking sheet with parchment paper. Combine almonds, sugar, egg whites, and vanilla extract in food processor and pulse until it has the texture of very coarse paste. Blend paste on high speed for 2 minutes, until very smooth and thick. Drop by spoonfuls onto baking sheet, forming 1-inch mounds. Allow batter to rest uncovered for 10 minutes. Bake at 400 degrees for 12 minutes. Allow to cool before dusting with powdered sugar.

YIELD: 8 SERVINGS

Fruitcake Cookies

- ½ cup shortening
- ½ cup butter
- 2 cups sugar
- 3 eggs
- 1 teaspoon vanilla
- 1 teaspoon lemon extract
- 3 cups flour
- ½ teaspoon salt
- 1 teaspoon baking soda
- ¾ teaspoon cinnamon
- 1 teaspoon allspice
- ¼ cup milk
- 2 cups chopped mixed dried fruit (dates, raisins, candied cherries, candied pineapple, citron)
- 1 cup chopped walnuts

Cream shortening, butter, and sugar. Add eggs and flavorings. Combine flour, salt, baking soda, and spices. Add alternately to creamed mixture along with milk. Stir in fruit and nuts. Drop by spoonfuls onto greased baking sheet at 350 degrees for 15 minutes.

YIELD: 5 TO 6 DOZEN

Christmas Tea Cookies

¾ cup shortening

Butter, use some with shortening to make ¾ cup

½ cup powdered sugar

1½ cups flour

¼ teaspoon salt

2 eggs, beaten

1 teaspoon vanilla

¼ cup chopped nuts (optional)

Powdered sugar

Cream together shortening, butter, and sugar. Combine dry ingredients and gently blend into creamed mixture. Don't overwork. Add beaten eggs and vanilla. Add nuts if desired. Chill dough for 2 hours, shape into balls, and roll in powdered sugar. Place on cookie sheet and flatten gently. Bake at 350 degrees for 20 minutes.

YIELD: 2 DOZEN

Holiday Spice Cookies

1¼ cups shortening
1 cup brown sugar
1 cup granulated sugar
3 eggs
3½ cups flour
1 teaspoon salt
1 teaspoon baking soda
1 teaspoon baking powder
1 teaspoon allspice
1 cup sour milk
1 teaspoon lemon juice (optional)

Cream together shortening, sugars, and eggs. Combine dry ingredients and add alternately to creamed mixture along with milk. Add lemon juice to milk if needed to sour it. Drop by spoonfuls onto greased cookie sheet and bake at 350 degrees for about 10 minutes.

YIELD: ABOUT 4 DOZEN

Molasses Pfeffernusse

- ¾ cup light molasses
- ½ cup butter
- 2 eggs, beaten
- 4 cups flour
- ½ cup sugar
- 1 teaspoon baking soda
- 2 teaspoons allspice
- ½ teaspoon salt
- ¼ teaspoon pepper
- Powdered sugar

Heat molasses and butter in saucepan to boiling for 30 seconds. Set aside to cool. Stir in eggs. Combine dry ingredients, except powdered sugar, in large bowl and add molasses mixture to it. Mix well and chill for 2 hours. Form dough into small balls. Bake on greased cookie sheet at 375 degrees for 10 minutes. Roll cookies in powdered sugar while still warm.

YIELD: 4 DOZEN

Gumdrop Gems

½ cup shortening
½ cup brown sugar
½ cup white sugar
1 egg
1 teaspoon vanilla
1½ cups flour
½ teaspoon baking powder
¼ teaspoon baking soda
½ teaspoon salt
½ cup moist flaked coconut
½ cup gumdrops (halved)

Cream together shortening, sugars, egg, and vanilla. Combine dry ingredients and add to creamed mixture. Fold in flaked coconut and mix well. Drop by spoonfuls onto ungreased cookie sheet. Place 1 gumdrop half in center of each cookie and bake at 350 degrees for 10 to 12 minutes.

YIELD: ABOUT 3 DOZEN

Mocha Kisses

- 2 cups semisweet chocolate chips, divided
- ½ cup shortening
- 1 cup brown sugar
- 1 egg
- 1 teaspoon vanilla
- ½ cup buttermilk
- 1½ cups flour
- 1 teaspoon baking soda
- ½ teaspoon salt
- ½ cup chopped nuts
- Chopped walnuts or pecans

Melt ½ cup chocolate chips and cream together with shortening, sugar, egg, vanilla, and buttermilk. Combine dry ingredients and add to creamed mixture. Fold in ½ cup nuts and rest of chocolate chips. Bake on greased cookie sheet at 350 degrees for 10 to 12 minutes. Frost with Mocha Buttercream Frosting (page 148). Sprinkle with chopped walnuts or pecans before frosting sets.

Yield: 3 dozen

Christmas Crackers

¼ cup butter
¼ cup shortening
¼ cup brown sugar
¼ cup granulated sugar
1 egg
1 teaspoon vanilla
1½ cups flour
½ teaspoon salt
½ teaspoon baking powder
½ teaspoon baking soda
1 cup chopped pecans

Cream together butter, shortening, sugars, egg, and vanilla. Combine dry ingredients and blend into creamed mixture. Add nuts and drop by spoonfuls onto ungreased cookie sheet. Bake at 350 degrees for about 10 minutes. Cookies will be flatter and crunchier than regular sugar cookies.

YIELD: 3 DOZEN

Peppermint Meringue Drops

4 egg whites
¼ teaspoon salt
¼ teaspoon cream of tartar
1 teaspoon peppermint extract
1½ cups sugar

With mixer, beat egg whites, salt, cream of tartar, and extract until soft peaks form. Add sugar gradually until mixture forms stiff peaks. Drop by spoonfuls onto parchment-lined cookie sheet. Bake at 300 degrees for about 20 minutes or until very lightly browned. Let meringues harden before removing from sheet. Serve with slivers of good quality semisweet chocolate.

YIELD: 1 TO 2 DOZEN

Coconut Oatmeal Cookies

1 cup shortening
½ cup butter
1 cup brown sugar
1 cup granulated sugar
1 teaspoon vanilla
2 eggs
2 cups flour
1 teaspoon salt
1 teaspoon baking soda
4 cups quick oats
1 cup flaked coconut

Cream together shortening, butter, sugars, vanilla, and eggs. Combine flour, salt, and soda and add to creamed mixture. Stir in oats and coconut. Drop by spoonfuls onto greased cookie sheet and bake at 350 degrees for 10 to 12 minutes.

Yield: 4 dozen

Old-Fashioned Sugar Cookies

1 cup vegetable oil
½ cup shortening
½ cup butter
1 cup sugar
1 cup brown sugar
2 eggs
1 teaspoon vanilla
1 teaspoon baking soda
4 cups flour
1 teaspoon cream of tartar
1 teaspoon salt
Granulated sugar

Cream oil, shortening, butter, and sugars. Blend in eggs and vanilla. Combine dry ingredients, except granulated sugar, and stir into creamed mixture. Dough will be soft. Form into 2-inch balls, roll in granulated sugar, and bake on greased cookie sheet at 350 degrees for 10 minutes.

YIELD: 3 TO 4 DOZEN

Orange Iced Cranberry Cookies

¾ cup sugar
½ cup brown sugar
½ cup softened butter
½ cup sour cream
1 teaspoon vanilla
2 eggs
2¼ cups flour
½ teaspoon baking soda
½ teaspoon baking powder
½ teaspoon salt
1 cup chopped fresh cranberries (dried cranberries work too)

Frosting

2 cups powdered sugar
2 tablespoons soft butter
1 teaspoon grated orange peel
2 to 3 tablespoons orange juice

In large bowl cream together sugars, butter, sour cream, vanilla, and eggs. Add dry ingredients and mix well. Stir in cranberries gently. Drop by spoonfuls onto lightly greased baking sheet and bake at 350 degrees for 12 minutes. Cool and top with orange frosting.

Yield: 3 dozen

Potato Chip Cookies

- 1 (14 ounce) can sweetened condensed milk
- ½ cup peanut butter
- 2 cups flaked coconut
- 1 cup crushed potato chips

Mix all ingredients. Bake on well-greased cookie sheet at 375 degrees for 8 to 10 minutes. Watch closely as cookies will easily burn.

YIELD: 1 TO 2 DOZEN

Sweet Tip:

Don't grease cookie sheets unless a recipe specifically tells you to do so.

Lemon Creams

½ cup shortening
¼ cup butter
1 cup sugar
1 egg
1 teaspoon lemon zest
1 tablespoon lemon pulp
2 tablespoons fresh lemon juice
2 cups flour
1 teaspoon baking soda
¼ teaspoon salt
Enough milk (if necessary) to make a soft dough
Coconut milk
Powdered sugar
Flaked coconut

Cream together shortening, butter, sugar, and egg. Mix together lemon zest, pulp, and juice and add alternately with combined dry ingredients to creamed mixture. Form into 1-inch balls and place on lightly greased cookie sheet. Press down lightly to form a disk. Brush with coconut milk and sprinkle very lightly with powdered sugar and a few strands of flaked coconut. Bake at 350 degrees for 10 to 12 minutes.

YIELD: 2 DOZEN

Sweet Tip:

Baking is fun when you're prepared! Get all your ingredients out and do the chopping, dicing, and measuring before you start. This way you'll know if you're missing something.

Most cookie dough may be frozen for up to 3 months. Drop dough onto greased sheets and freeze; bag the frozen dough, keep it in the freezer, and pull out as much as you need for an anytime quick batch of cookies!

Bar Cookies

From elegant to simple, bar desserts are rich with layers of flavor and variety. They are baked in the same pan from which they can be cut up and served and make for easy transport to your next Christmas gathering. Bars tend to be heartier and more substantial, so one pan is usually enough for even a sizable group. Like cookies, they're eaten by hand, but a few recipes are softer and suitable for serving on a dessert plate topped with ice cream or whipped cream.

Sweet Tip:

The yield for bar cookies varies greatly depending on the richness of the ingredients. A good rule of thumb: A 9x9-inch baking dish will yield 12 to 16 bars, and a 9x13-inch pan will yield 16 to 20 bars.

Cranberry Paradise Bars

2½ cups flour
2½ teaspoons baking powder
⅓ teaspoon salt
¼ cup softened butter
½ cup shortening
1¾ cups brown sugar
3 large eggs
1 teaspoon vanilla
½ teaspoon orange flavoring
½ cup orange-flavored dried cranberries
½ cup white chocolate chips

Sift together flour, baking powder, and salt and set aside. Beat butter, shortening, and brown sugar together until creamy. Beat in eggs, vanilla, and orange flavoring. Add flour mixture in ½ cup increments, mixing well. Stir in dried cranberries and white chocolate chips. Spread into greased jelly roll pan and bake at 350 degrees for 20 minutes or until golden brown. Cool completely and cut into bars.

7-Layer Bars

- 1 stick butter
- 1 cup graham cracker crumbs
- 1 cup milk chocolate chips
- 1 cup butterscotch chips
- 1 cup semisweet chocolate chips
- 1 cup shredded coconut
- 1 cup pecans (chopped)
- 1 (14 ounce) can sweetened condensed milk

Melt butter in 8x8-inch baking pan. Stir in graham cracker crumbs and pat evenly in bottom. Sprinkle other ingredients, except milk, over crumbs in layers. Pour milk evenly over the top. Bake at 350 degrees for 25 to 30 minutes. Let cool and cut into bars.

Sweet Tip:

As long as they are covered tightly, bar cookies store best in the container in which they were baked. Cut out only as many bars as you need, then reseal immediately.

Cloud Nine Butterscotch Squares

½ cup butter or margarine
1 small box instant butterscotch pudding mix
2 eggs, beaten
1 teaspoon vanilla
1 cup flour
1 teaspoon baking powder
½ teaspoon salt
½ cup milk
1 cup old-fashioned oatmeal (uncooked)
1 cup semisweet chocolate chips

Cream together butter and pudding mix. Beat until light and fluffy. Add eggs and vanilla. Combine flour, baking powder, and salt. Add alternately with milk. Fold in oats and chocolate chips. Spread batter evenly in greased 9-inch square pan and bake at 350 degrees for 20 to 25 minutes.

Sweet Tip:

Buy cheap plastic shower caps in bulk at the local dollar store and use them for quick stretch-to-fit covers on pans of bars or over a plate of cookies for transport or storage.

Lemon Bars

1 cup flour
½ cup butter or margarine
¼ cup powdered sugar
2 eggs
2 tablespoons flour
1 cup sugar
3 tablespoons lemon juice
½ teaspoon salt
½ teaspoon baking powder
Powdered sugar

Blend flour, butter, and powdered sugar and press into 8x11-inch pan. Bake at 350 degrees for 15 minutes. While that's baking, combine next six ingredients and mix until smooth. Pour over crust and bake at 350 degrees for 20 to 25 minutes. Sprinkle powdered sugar on top. Cut into squares while still warm.

Spicy Nut Triangles

1 cup margarine
1 cup sugar
1 egg (separated)
2 cups flour
1 teaspoon cinnamon
1 cup finely chopped walnuts

Cream together margarine and sugar. Add egg yolk and beat well. Add flour and cinnamon. Spread evenly in jelly roll pan (15x10-inch). Beat egg white slightly and brush over batter with fingertips. Sprinkle nuts over batter and gently press them in. Bake in a slow oven (275 degrees) for about an hour. While still warm, cut into 4 lengthwise strips and 6 crosswise strips. Then cut each piece in half diagonally. (These freeze well.)

YIELD: 48 TRIANGLES

Crème de Menthe Squares

- 1¼ cups real butter, divided
- ½ cup cocoa
- 3½ cups powdered sugar, divided
- 1 teaspoon vanilla
- 2 cups graham cracker crumbs
- ⅓ cup crème de menthe
- 1½ cups semisweet chocolate chips

In heavy saucepan combine ½ cup of butter with cocoa. Heat and whisk until well blended. Remove from heat and add ½ cup powdered sugar. Stir in vanilla and cracker crumbs. Mix well and place in greased 9x13-inch baking pan. Then melt ½ cup butter and combine in small bowl with crème de menthe. At low speed, beat in 3 cups powdered sugar. Spread over bottom layer. Chill 1 hour. Then combine ¼ cup butter and chocolate chips. Stir over low heat until melted. Spread over mint layer. Chill 1 to 2 hours. Remove from refrigerator 15 minutes prior to serving. This will prevent top layer from breaking when squares are cut.

Sweet Tip:

Give a gift of sweet treats from your kitchen this holiday season. Wrap a stack of fresh, homemade cookies with red and green plastic wrap and secure with a festive ribbon.

Toffee Bars

2 sticks butter
1 cup dark brown sugar
1 egg
1 teaspoon vanilla
2 cups flour
1 cup chocolate chips
½ cup chopped pecans

Cream butter and sugar. Add egg and vanilla. Mix well. Add flour and blend well. Spread ¼-inch thick in jelly roll pan, leaving about ½ inch of space around the edges. Bake at 350 degrees for 15 minutes. Immediately after removing from oven, sprinkle chocolate chips evenly over the top. Let stand for 2 minutes and then gently spread melted chocolate around. Sprinkle nuts all over and let cool. Cut into small bars.

Mincemeat Bars

¼ cup shortening
¾ cup sugar
2 eggs
¾ cup mincemeat
½ cup drained, crushed pineapple (save juice)
1½ cups nuts
1½ cups flour
½ teaspoon salt
½ teaspoon cinnamon
¼ teaspoon baking soda

Cream shortening, sugar, and eggs. Add mincemeat, pineapple, and nuts. Combine dry ingredients and add to creamed mixture. Spread into 9x13-inch pan and bake at 350 degrees for 30 minutes. Top with frosting.

Frosting

1½ cups powdered sugar
2 tablespoons butter
1½ tablespoons hot pineapple juice
Pinch salt

Sweet Tip:

An ideal cookie-cooling station in wintertime? A table on your porch.

Rudolph's Apple Bars

- 2 cups sugar
- 1 cup vegetable oil
- 3 eggs, beaten
- 3 cups flour
- 1 teaspoon baking soda
- 1 teaspoon salt
- 1 teaspoon cinnamon
- 1 cup chopped nuts
- 3 large cored and diced red apples (with skins)
- 2 teaspoons vanilla

Cream sugar and oil. Add beaten eggs. Combine flour, soda, salt, and cinnamon and add to creamed mixture. Fold in nuts, apples, and vanilla. Bake in 9x13-inch greased and floured pan at 350 degrees for about 30 minutes.

Peanut Jelly Bars

- ¾ cup butter
- 1 cup brown sugar
- 1½ cups flour
- 1 teaspoon salt
- ½ teaspoon baking soda
- 1½ cups quick oats
- ½ cup chopped peanuts
- 1¼ cups strawberry or grape jelly

Cream together butter and sugar until light and fluffy. Add combined dry ingredients and mix well. Stir in oats and nuts. Press half crumb mixture into bottom of greased 9x13-inch pan. Spread with jelly and top with remaining crumb mixture. Bake at 400 degrees for 20 to 25 minutes. Cool and cut into bars.

Banana Bars

¾ cup shortening
1 mashed banana
¾ cup sugar
1 egg
1½ cups flour
½ teaspoon salt
½ teaspoon baking powder
¼ teaspoon baking soda
¾ teaspoon cinnamon
¼ teaspoon allspice
¼ cup milk
½ cup chopped nuts

Cream shortening, banana, sugar, and egg. Combine dry ingredients and add alternately to creamed mixture along with milk. Add nuts. Bake in 9x13-inch pan at 350 degrees for about 20 minutes. Ice with Buttercream Frosting (page 148) while still slightly warm. Cool and cut into bars.

Sweet Tip:

Before you start baking, sit down with your recipe cards and grocery list and jot down ingredients you're missing. Nothing spoils the enjoyment of baking faster than discovering halfway through prep that you're missing a crucial ingredient!

Peanut Crispy Bars

- ¼ cup butter
- 5 cups miniature marshmallows
- ⅓ cup peanut butter
- 5 cups crispy rice cereal
- 1 cup dry roasted peanuts

Melt butter in microwave. Add marshmallows and microwave for 2 minutes or until very soft, stirring occasionally to encourage melting. Remove from microwave and stir in peanut butter, cereal, and peanuts. Press warm mixture into lightly buttered 8x12-inch dish. Cool and cut into bars.

YIELD: ABOUT 36 BARS

Angel Bars

1 cup flour
4 tablespoons powdered sugar
½ cup melted butter
1 cup sugar
1 teaspoon baking powder
¼ teaspoon salt
3 beaten eggs
3 tablespoons lemon juice
1 tablespoon lemon zest
¾ cup flaked coconut
Powdered sugar

Combine first three ingredients and press into 9x9-inch square baking dish. Bake at 350 degrees for 15 minutes. Then combine remaining ingredients, except powdered sugar, together and pour over slightly cooled crust. Bake another 20 minutes at 350 degrees. Sprinkle with powdered sugar when cool, then cut into bars.

Sweet Tip:

Don't allow the stress that so often accompanies the holidays to steal your joy. Remember the reason for the season! Fix yourself a nice cup of tea, grab a fabulous cookie, then find a quiet corner to relax, open your Bible, and read through the account of Christ's birth in the second chapter of Luke. It will help you refocus on the important things.

Yummy Pie Bars

- $1\frac{3}{4}$ cups graham cracker crumbs
- $\frac{1}{4}$ cup sugar
- $\frac{1}{2}$ teaspoon salt
- $\frac{1}{3}$ cup butter, melted
- 1 pint whipping cream
- $\frac{1}{2}$ cup sugar
- 1 (10 ounce) bag miniature marshmallows
- 1 can blueberry or cherry pie filling
- Whipped cream

Mix together cracker crumbs, $\frac{1}{4}$ cup sugar, salt, and melted butter. Pat into a 9x13-inch pan and put in freezer for 10 minutes. Whip cream until stiff. Mix with $\frac{1}{2}$ cup sugar and marshmallows. Pour over crust. Spoon pie filling over the top and refrigerate overnight. Cut into bars and serve with whipped cream.

Turtle Bars

- 1 box German chocolate cake mix
- ¾ cup melted butter
- ⅔ cup evaporated milk, divided
- 1 bag caramels
- 1 cup milk chocolate chips
- 1 cup chopped pecans

Combine cake mix with butter and ⅓ cup evaporated milk. Press half of mix in greased 9x13-inch pan. (Reserve other half for top.) Bake at 350 degrees for 10 minutes. Melt caramels in remaining ⅓ cup evaporated milk. Sprinkle chocolate chips on cake right after removing it from oven. Pour caramel over all, sprinkle nuts on top, and finish by dropping spoonfuls of remaining cake mix on top. Spread as best you can. Bake at 350 degrees for 20 minutes. Cool and cut into bars.

Almond Nut Bars

- 1 (16 ounce) bag marshmallows
- ½ cup milk
- 1 teaspoon vanilla
- 2 cups whipped topping
- 1 (8 ounce) chocolate almond bar, shaved
- 2 cups graham cracker crumbs, divided

Heat marshmallows and milk until completely melted. Cool well and add vanilla. Fold in whipped topping and chocolate shavings. Press 1 cup graham cracker crumbs into 8x8-inch pan. Pour in filling and top with second cup of cracker crumbs. Refrigerate until well set. Cut into bars.

Fudge Brownies

½ cup butter
2 (1 ounce) squares unsweetened chocolate
1 cup sugar
2 eggs
1 teaspoon vanilla
1 cup flour
½ teaspoon baking powder
½ teaspoon salt
½ cup chopped walnuts
Powdered sugar

Melt butter and chocolate over low heat. Remove from heat and stir in sugar. Add eggs and vanilla; beat just until blended. Stir in flour, baking powder, salt, and nuts. Spread batter in 8x8-inch baking pan and bake at 350 degrees for 30 minutes. When cool, sprinkle lightly with powdered sugar.

Yield: 16 brownies

Sweet Tip:

When preparing a recipe of any kind, clean up as you go. Having a medium-sized bowl or plastic grocery bag on the prep counter (for eggshells, wrappers, sticky spoons and spatulas, and peelings) will keep your work space clutter-free and make cleanup a snap!

Butterscotch Brownies

¼ cup shortening
1 cup brown sugar
1 egg
1 cup flour
½ teaspoon baking powder
½ teaspoon salt
½ teaspoon vanilla
½ cup chopped nuts

Cream together shortening and sugar. Add egg. Combine flour, baking powder, and salt. Stir in vanilla and nuts. Spread in well-greased 8x8-inch baking dish and bake at 350 degrees for 20 to 25 minutes.

Shepherd Boy Toffee

Saltine crackers
1 cup brown sugar
2 sticks real butter
1 (12 ounce) bag chocolate chips

Line cookie sheet with foil. Lightly coat with butter, then put down a layer of saltine crackers. Mix brown sugar and butter in saucepan and bring to boil for 3 minutes. Spread on top of crackers and bake at 400 degrees for 5 minutes. Remove pan from oven and immediately sprinkle with chocolate chips. Wait until chips are very soft and then spread evenly with spatula. Refrigerate and cut into bars. Tastes just like toffee candy bars!

Rhubarb Squares

3 cups flour
½ teaspoon salt
¾ cup brown sugar
1½ cups butter
1 cup quick oats
1 teaspoon cinnamon
½ cup brown sugar

Filling

2½ cups rhubarb, sliced small
½ cup water
½ cup sugar
Dash salt

Combine first four ingredients for crust. Reserve ⅓ of the mixture. Spread remaining ⅔ in 9x13-inch pan. Press down. Mix filling ingredients in saucepan and simmer for 20 minutes, or until soft. Pour into blender and puree. Pour over crust. Combine oatmeal, cinnamon, and brown sugar with remaining crust mixture and sprinkle over fruit. Bake at 400 degrees for 25 minutes or until bubbling. Cool and cut into bars. Great served warm with ice cream!

Oatmeal Carmelitas

2 cups flour
2 cups quick oats
1½ cups brown sugar
1 teaspoon baking soda
½ teaspoon salt
1¼ cups butter

Filling

1 cup caramel ice cream topping
3 tablespoons flour
1 cup semisweet chocolate chips
½ cup chopped nuts

Blend crust ingredients until crumbly. Press ½ of crumb mixture in bottom of 9x13-inch pan. Reserve remaining crumbs for topping. Bake at 350 degrees for 10 minutes. Combine caramel topping and flour. Remove partially baked crust from oven and sprinkle with chocolate chips and nuts. Drizzle evenly with caramel mixture and sprinkle with reserved crumbs. Continue baking for another 20 minutes. Cool completely, then refrigerate for 2 hours. Cut into bars.

Coconut Delight Bars

- 3 cups butter cracker crumbs
- 1½ cups butter
- 1½ cups whole sweet milk
- 3 small packages coconut instant pudding
- ½ gallon vanilla ice cream, softened
- 8 ounces whipped topping

Mix cracker crumbs and butter and press ½ of crumb mixture into 9x13-inch pan. (Reserve rest for topping.) Mix milk and pudding. Stir in softened ice cream and whipped topping until well blended. Pour over crust and top with remaining crumbs. Chill and serve. You'll need a dessert plate for this bar!

Orange Slice Bars

1 pound orange candy slices
2 cups flour
½ teaspoon salt
3 cups brown sugar
4 eggs, slightly beaten
1 cup chopped nuts
1 teaspoon vanilla
Granulated sugar (optional)

Using scissors, cut orange slices into small pieces. Add to flour and salt. Add remaining ingredients and mix well. Spread in two greased 9x9-inch baking pans and bake at 350 degrees for 45 minutes. After pans are taken from oven, sprinkle with granulated sugar, if desired. Cut into bars.

Sweet Tip:

Use all-purpose flour in cookie baking. Don't sift it unless the recipe specifically tells you to.

Pumpkin Bars

1 cup vegetable oil
2 cups sugar
2 cups canned pumpkin
4 eggs
2 teaspoons cinnamon
½ teaspoon salt
1 teaspoon baking soda
2 teaspoons baking powder
2 cups flour

Frosting

3 ounces cream cheese, softened
1 teaspoon vanilla
¾ stick butter, softened
1 tablespoon cream or milk
1¾ cups powdered sugar

Cream oil and sugar. Add remaining ingredients. Pour into greased jelly roll pan and bake at 350 degrees for 25 minutes. Cool. Cream together frosting ingredients and frost. Cut into bars.

Raspberry Bars

- 1 cup butter
- 1½ cups sugar, divided
- 2 egg yolks
- 2½ cups flour
- 10 ounces raspberry jam
- 4 egg whites
- 1½ cups finely chopped walnuts

Cream butter with ½ cup sugar. Beat in egg yolks and gradually stir in part of the flour. With fingers, work in remaining flour until smooth dough is formed. Pat into ungreased jelly roll pan and bake at 350 degrees until firm but not brown, about 15 minutes. Remove from oven and spread with jam. Set aside. Beat egg whites until foamy, then add remaining sugar and beat until stiff peaks form. Fold in nuts and spread over jam. Bake at 350 degrees until meringue is firm, 20 to 25 minutes. Meringue will crack. While still warm, loosen edges and cut into bars.

North Pole Gingerbread Bars

- 1 cup brown sugar
- ½ cup shortening
- 1 cup molasses
- 2 teaspoons baking soda
- 1 cup boiling water
- 3 cups flour
- 1 teaspoon ginger
- 1 teaspoon cinnamon
- 1 teaspoon allspice
- 1 teaspoon nutmeg
- 1 teaspoon cloves
- ½ teaspoon salt
- 2 well-beaten eggs
- Whipped cream (optional)

Blend brown sugar and shortening. Add molasses and mix well. Add baking soda to boiling water. Hold the cup over the bowl so the foam from the water/baking soda reaction will go into the bowl of creamed mixture. Pour in remaining water and mix well. Combine dry ingredients and mix with creamed mixture. Add eggs and mix well. Bake in greased 9x13-inch baking pan at 350 degrees for 30 minutes. Cool and cut into bars. Best served with whipped cream.

Triple-Decker Chocolate Squares

- ½ cup butter
- ¼ cup cocoa
- ½ cup powdered sugar
- ½ teaspoon salt
- 1 egg, beaten
- 1½ teaspoons vanilla
- 3 cups graham cracker crumbs
- ½ cup chopped pecans
- 1 teaspoon cornstarch
- 1 tablespoon sugar
- ¼ cup butter, melted
- ¼ cup evaporated milk
- 1 teaspoon vanilla
- 2 cups powdered sugar
- 1 (8 ounce) milk chocolate bar, shaved

Melt ½ cup butter and add next seven ingredients and cook until hot and well blended. Press into lightly buttered 9x13-inch pan and set aside. Combine cornstarch and 1 tablespoon sugar and add to ¼ cup melted butter in heavy saucepan. Mix well. Add milk and cook until thick and creamy. When cool, add 1 teaspoon vanilla and 2 cups powdered sugar. Blend well and spread over first layer. Melt chocolate bar and drizzle over cream filling. Cut into bars before chocolate is hardened.

Raisin Bars with Cinnamon Glaze

1 stick butter
1 cup brown sugar
1½ cups flour
½ teaspoon baking soda
½ teaspoon salt
1 tablespoon water
1½ cups quick oats
1½ cups raisin filling
½ teaspoon cinnamon

Filling

1 cup raisins
¼ cup sugar
1 tablespoon cornstarch
1 cup water

Cream together butter and sugar. Combine flour, baking soda, and salt and add to creamed mixture. Add water and oats. Press half of crumb mixture into 9x13-inch baking pan. Cook raisins in saucepan with sugar, cornstarch, and water until thick. Spread raisin filling over crumb layer. Top with remaining crumb mixture and bake at 350 degrees about 30 minutes. Glaze with very thin Buttercream Frosting mixed with ½ teaspoon cinnamon (page 148).

Almond Joy Bars

15 graham crackers, broken into small chunks

1 (14 ounce) can sweetened condensed milk

1 cup semisweet chocolate chips

1 cup flaked coconut

½ cup chopped almonds, toasted

Dash salt

Mix all ingredients together and bake in greased 8x8-inch baking pan at 350 degrees for about 30 minutes. Cut into bars while still warm.

White Chocolate Wonder Bars

- 1½ cups flour
- ½ teaspoon baking powder
- ¼ teaspoon salt
- ½ stick butter
- 2 cups white chocolate chips, divided
- ¾ cup sugar
- 3 eggs
- 2 teaspoons vanilla
- 1 cup semisweet chocolate chips
- 1 cup chopped macadamia nuts

Combine flour, baking powder, and salt. Melt butter in small saucepan. Don't boil. Remove from heat and add 1 cup white chocolate chips. Leave sitting to melt without stirring. Beat together sugar, eggs, and vanilla until creamy. Add butter mixture and blend gently. Stir in flour mixture. Fold in remaining white and semisweet chocolate chips along with nuts. Spread batter in 9x9-inch greased and parchment-lined baking pan. Bake at 325 degrees for about 25 minutes or just until set. Cool and cut into bars.

Sweet Tip:

Volunteer to bake cookies for college kids you know. The weeks between Thanksgiving and Christmas are when they're cramming for exams, staying up late to study and finish papers. Having ziplock bags of cookies on their desks will spur them on and help them finish the semester well.

Glazed Apple Bars

½ cup lukewarm milk
2 eggs
2 teaspoons instant yeast
4 cups flour
½ teaspoon salt
2 sticks butter
8 cups thinly sliced
  Granny Smith apples
¾ cup sugar
¼ cup cornstarch
Dash salt
2 teaspoons cinnamon

GLAZE

1 cup powdered sugar
2 tablespoons milk
1 teaspoon vanilla
Dash salt

Beat milk and eggs together and set aside. Combine yeast, flour, and ½ teaspoon salt. Cut in butter with pastry blender until mixture forms coarse pastry crumbs. Add egg mixture, blending until soft dough forms. Divide in half and roll out one of the halves into a rectangle and place on greased cookie sheet. Spread apple slices over dough. Combine sugar, cornstarch, dash of salt, and cinnamon. Sprinkle over apples. Roll out remaining dough and place over apples, crimping edges. Cut steam vents in top crust. Cover and put in warm place away from drafts for about 1 hour to rise. Bake at 350 degrees for 25 minutes. Glaze when slightly warm. Cool completely before cutting into squares.

Chocolate Pizza

- 1 cup shortening
- 1 cup brown sugar
- ½ cup white sugar
- 2 eggs
- 1 teaspoon vanilla
- 2¼ cups flour
- 1 teaspoon baking soda
- ½ teaspoon salt
- Assorted candy bars, roughly chopped into chunks

Cream together shortening, sugars, eggs, and vanilla. Combine flour, soda, and salt. Stir into creamed mixture. Press cookie dough into greased 9x9-inch baking pan and bake at 350 degrees for 15 to 20 minutes. As soon as baked dough is removed from oven, spread thick layer of chopped candy bars over it. Return to oven for 5 minutes. Turn off oven but leave pan in for 10 minutes or until candy bars are melted but still slightly chunky. Remove from oven. When nearly cool and before candy hardens again, cut into bars. Really, anything goes with this recipe. Use any of your favorite candy bars and enjoy!

Praline Bars

24 graham crackers
(double rectangles)

¾ stick butter

¾ stick margarine

1 cup light brown sugar

Dash salt

1 cup chopped pecans

Place graham crackers as close as possible on greased jelly roll pan. Boil butter, margarine, sugar, and salt for 2 minutes. Remove from heat and add pecans. Immediately spread over graham crackers and bake at 350 degrees for 10 minutes. Watch carefully to avoid burning. When cool, break into pieces and store in airtight container.

Strawberry Bars

- ¾ pound vanilla wafers, crushed, divided
- 1 (14 ounce) can sweetened condensed milk
- 1¼ cups chopped pecans
- 1 (12 ounce) container whipped topping, divided
- 1 (16 ounce) carton frozen strawberries, partially thawed

Spread ¾ of vanilla wafers on the bottom of 9x13-inch pan. Drizzle milk over crust. Sprinkle with pecans. Spread with half of whipped topping. Spread partially thawed berries over whipped topping. Top with remaining whipped topping and sprinkle remainder of wafer crumbs on top. Freeze. Take out 1 hour prior to serving. Cut into bars and serve on dessert plate. You'll need a fork for this one!

Cheesecake Bars

⅓ cup chopped nuts
⅓ cup brown sugar
⅔ cup flour
4 tablespoons butter

Filling

1 (8 ounce) package cream cheese, softened
¼ cup sugar
1 egg
2 tablespoons cream
1 tablespoon lemon juice
½ teaspoon vanilla
¼ teaspoon salt

Combine first four ingredients for crust and press into bottom of 8x8-inch baking pan. Bake at 350 for 12 minutes. With mixer, cream together cream cheese, sugar, and egg. Add cream, lemon juice, vanilla, and salt. Beat until frothy and pour into baked crust. Bake at 350 degrees for 20 minutes. Refrigerate and cut into bars to serve.

Maple Bars

½ cup butter
1¾ cups brown sugar
2 eggs
1 teaspoon maple flavoring
1½ cups flour
2 teaspoons baking powder
½ cup nuts

Cream together butter and sugar. Add egg and flavoring. Combine flour and baking powder and blend into creamed mixture; fold in nuts. Bake at 350 degrees in greased 9x9-inch baking pan for 25 to 30 minutes. Cool and cut into bars.

No-Bake Cookies

Like their name, no-bakes never require an oven. A number of steps and additional pieces of equipment are usually omitted as well, but careful attention to stovetop cooking times and ingredient measurements is essential for success. Experiment a bit (when you're not under pressure) with cooking temperatures on your stove, with your equipment, in your altitude, and make notations on the recipes as you try them.

Apricot Balls

- 1 (8 ounce) package dried apricots, finely diced
- 2½ cups flaked coconut
- ¾ cup sweetened condensed milk
- 1 cup finely chopped nuts (pecans work very well)

Mix together apricots, coconut, and milk. Shape into 1-inch balls and roll in nuts. Refrigerate.

YIELD: 2 DOZEN

Sweet Tip:

Remember, the higher the quality of your ingredients, the higher the quality of the finished product!

Winter Haystacks

1½ cups semisweet chocolate chips
½ cup peanut butter
½ cup peanuts
2½ cups chow mein noodles (uncooked)

Melt chocolate and stir in peanut butter and nuts. Stir in noodles. Drop by tablespoons onto wax paper and let harden.

YIELD: 2 DOZEN

Christmas Bark

- 1 pound almond bark or white chocolate
- ¾ cup dried cranberries
- 1 (3 to 4 ounce) jar macadamia nuts

Melt bark or chocolate in microwave or double broiler. Stir in cranberries and nuts. Pour into jelly roll pan lined with foil and spread evenly. Refrigerate 1 hour, then break into pieces.

Krispy Kringles

- 1 stick butter
- 1 cup dates (chopped)
- 1 cup sugar
- 1 egg
- 2 cups crisp rice cereal
- ½ cup chopped walnuts
- ½ cup coconut

Mix together butter, dates, sugar, and egg. Heat just to bubbling and cook for 4 minutes. Remove from heat and add cereal and nuts. Mix well. When cool enough to handle, roll into balls, and then roll in coconut.

YIELD: 3 DOZEN

Pastels

2 eggs, beaten
1½ sticks butter
1 cup sugar
1 tablespoon vanilla
2 cups graham cracker crumbs
2 cups chopped nuts
1 cup flaked coconut
2½ cups colored miniature marshmallows
Powdered sugar

Cook first three ingredients over medium heat until thickened. Cool; add vanilla and set aside. In large bowl combine cracker crumbs, nuts, coconut, and marshmallows. Pour cooked, cooled mixture over remainder of ingredients. Mix well. Press into buttered pan and refrigerate for 2 hours. Cut and roll in powdered sugar. Store in refrigerator.

YIELD: 3 TO 4 DOZEN

Sweet Tip:

For very best results, always use real, high-quality butter when it's called for.

Chocolate Jumbles

- 2 cups sugar
- 3 tablespoons cocoa
- ½ cup butter or margarine
- ½ cup milk
- ¼ teaspoon salt
- 3 cups quick oats
- 1 teaspoon vanilla

In heavy saucepan, bring sugar, cocoa, butter, milk, and salt to a rapid boil. Boil for 1 minute. Add oats and vanilla and mix well. Working quickly, drop by spoonfuls onto wax paper. Cookies will set up as they cool.

YIELD: 2 DOZEN

Butterscotch Tassies

1 cup butterscotch chips
2 tablespoons peanut butter
3 cups cornflakes

Melt butterscotch chips and peanut butter together. Add cornflakes and mix well. Drop by spoonfuls onto wax paper and cool.

YIELD: 2 TO 3 DOZEN

Pretzel Cookies

1 cup butterscotch chips
1 cup milk chocolate chips
1 cup dry roasted peanuts
1 cup broken-up pretzel sticks

Melt chips in saucepan. Stir in peanuts and pretzels and drop by mounds onto wax paper. Refrigerate to harden.

YIELD: 2 DOZEN

Ritzy Bits

Crunchy peanut butter
Butter crackers
2 cups chocolate chips
Small amount of milk (optional)
1 tablespoon butter (optional)

Sandwich crunchy peanut butter between two butter crackers. Melt chocolate chips in saucepan. You may add small amount of milk and tablespoon of butter to make good dipping mixture. Coat cracker cookies with chocolate and let them harden on wax paper.

Sweet Tip:

Grown-ups can get mighty harried at holiday time. Plan a date night with your sweetheart right smack in the middle of the season—when a favorite restaurant is decorated for Christmas. Or make a date with good friends. Make your reservation plenty early, and get a sitter well in advance of the evening—they get snapped up quickly this time of year!

Snow Fudgies

2 cups sugar
1 cup evaporated milk
Dash salt
1 stick butter
1 cup white chocolate chips
½ cup flaked coconut
½ cup chopped pecans
1 teaspoon vanilla

In heavy saucepan, cook sugar, milk, salt, and butter over medium heat to 238 degrees on candy thermometer, stirring constantly. Remove from heat and let stand 10 minutes. Add white chocolate and stir until melted. Quickly add in coconut, pecans, and vanilla. Spread into buttered 8x8-inch pan. Cool and cut into squares.

YIELD: 16 SQUARES

Chocolate Nut Chews

- 1½ cups sugar
- ¼ cup cocoa
- ⅓ cup peanut butter
- ½ cup evaporated milk
- ⅓ cup butter
- 1½ cups quick oats
- ½ cup salted cashews
- 1 teaspoon vanilla

Combine first five ingredients in saucepan and bring to boil. Boil for two minutes. Remove from heat and stir in oats, nuts, and vanilla. Drop by large spoonfuls onto wax paper and allow to harden.

YIELD: 2 TO 3 DOZEN

Christmas Corn Crunch

3 quarts popped corn
3 cups corn cereal squares
3 cups broken-up corn chips
1 (10 ounce) package peanut butter or butterscotch chips
1 (10 ounce) package milk or dark chocolate chips

In large bowl, combine popcorn, cereal, and corn chips. In saucepan over medium heat, melt peanut butter chips and chocolate chips. Stir until smooth. Pour over popcorn mixture and toss to coat. Spread onto 2 greased baking sheets. Cool and break into pieces.

Truffle Cookies

- 1 package chocolate sandwich cookies, crushed
- 1 (8 ounce) package cream cheese, softened
- 2 cups semisweet chocolate chips, melted
- 1 cup white chocolate chips, melted

In large bowl, combine crushed cookies and cream cheese to form stiff dough. Shape into 1½-inch balls. Using a fork, dip balls into melted chocolate. Place on wire rack over wax paper in a cool area until set. Drizzle with melted white chocolate.

YIELD: 2 DOZEN

Maraschino Cherry Balls

- ½ cup butter, melted
- 6 tablespoons light corn syrup
- 1 (14 ounce) can sweetened condensed milk
- 1 teaspoon vanilla
- Dash salt
- 3 pounds powdered sugar
- 3 (10 ounce) jars maraschino cherries, drained
- 2 cups semisweet chocolate chips
- ½ tablespoon butter

In large bowl, combine ½ cup butter, corn syrup, condensed milk, vanilla, salt, and sugar. Knead dough and form into walnut-sized balls with a cherry wrapped in middle. Place in freezer to chill. Melt chocolate chips and ½ tablespoon butter. Dip chilled balls in chocolate and let them set up on wax or parchment paper.

YIELD: 2 TO 3 DOZEN

Chocolate Fruit Balls

- ½ cup dried apricots, chopped
- ½ cup dried cranberries, chopped
- 1 (8 ounce) bar milk chocolate, shaved
- 1 cup dark or white chocolate
- ¼ cup butter

Combine fruit and chocolate shavings. Form into small balls and refrigerate overnight. Melt chocolates with butter and stir until smooth. Dip chilled balls in chocolate and let set up on wax or parchment paper.

YIELD: 1 TO 2 DOZEN

Vanilla Bark Cookies

- 1 pound vanilla bark or white chocolate chips
- ½ cup crunchy peanut butter
- 1 cup crisp rice cereal
- 1 cup miniature marshmallows
- 1 cup dry roasted nuts

Break up bark and melt it with peanut butter in microwave on medium setting. Pour over other ingredients and mix well. Drop by spoonfuls onto wax paper to harden.

YIELD: 2 DOZEN

Rolled Cookies

By far the most popular cookies at Christmastime are rollouts! Kids love getting in the act and indulging their creativity with the many colors and shapes of toppings available for decoration. It's a sloppy, sticky, fun, and laughter-filled activity for the whole family that generally involves lots of frosting and clumsy fingers! Messy. . .but worth it!

Sweet Tip:

Chilled dough needs to sit at room temperature for about 30 minutes to make it perfect for rolling out.

Christmas Rollouts

- 1 cup shortening
- 2 cups sugar
- 2 eggs
- ½ cup sweetened condensed milk
- 1 teaspoon soda
- ½ teaspoon salt
- 1 teaspoon baking powder
- 1 teaspoon lemon flavoring
- 5 cups flour

Cream together shortening and sugar; add eggs and milk. Mix well. Combine next five ingredients and blend into creamed mixture. Roll ¼ of the dough at a time, as gently as possible to prevent dough from becoming tough, to about ¼ inch. Cut out shapes with cookie cutters and bake on greased cookie sheet at 350 degrees for 8 to 10 minutes. Cool. Frost with Buttercream Icing (see recipe on page 148) and decorate.

YIELD: 4 DOZEN

Gingerbread Men

1 cup brown sugar
⅓ cup shortening
1½ cups dark molasses
⅔ cup water
7 cups flour
2 teaspoons baking soda
2 teaspoons ginger
1 teaspoon salt
1 teaspoon allspice
1 teaspoon cloves
1 teaspoon cinnamon

Mix brown sugar, shortening, molasses, and water. Stir in remaining ingredients. Cover and refrigerate about 2 hours. Roll out ¼ of the dough at a time to ½-inch thickness. Cut with gingerbread man cookie cutter and place cookies on lightly greased cookie sheet. Leave plenty of room between each cookie so they will bake without touching. Bake at 350 degrees for 10 to 12 minutes. Cool, frost, and decorate.

YIELD: 3 DOZEN

Bizcochos, Mexican Holiday Cookies

2 cups shortening or 1 pound lard
1 cup sugar
1 egg
1 teaspoon vanilla
1 teaspoon baking soda
½ teaspoon ground cloves
1 teaspoon cinnamon
½ teaspoon ground anise powder
5 cups flour
1 teaspoon salt
Juice of one orange
1 cup powdered sugar
3 tablespoons cinnamon

Cream together shortening and sugar. Add egg and vanilla and mix well. Combine next six ingredients and add to shortening mixture, ½ to 1 cup at a time. Add orange juice and mix thoroughly. Roll out on floured surface and cut into desired shapes. Bake at 325 to 350 degrees for 8 minutes, or until golden brown. Cool and then dust with mixture of powdered sugar and cinnamon.

YIELD: 4 DOZEN

Sweet Tip:

Use a small resealable plastic bag as a cookie icing decorator and drizzler. Fill, release air, and lock bag. Cut an appropriate-sized hole in one of the lower corners and squeeze gently to decorate.

Auntie Annie's Almond Cookies

1 cup butter
½ cup sugar
1 egg
½ teaspoon almond extract
2½ cups flour

Frosting

½ stick butter
2 to 3 cups powdered sugar
½ teaspoon almond extract
Milk

Cream together butter and sugar. Add egg and extract. Add flour all at once and blend, but don't overmix. Chill for 1 hour. Roll out to ½-inch thickness and cut out as you desire. Bake on lightly greased cookie sheet at 350 degrees for 10 to 12 minutes. To make almond cookie frosting, blend ingredients together, adding milk one tablespoon at a time until you reach desired consistency.

Yield: 2 dozen

Poppy Seed Cookies

½ cup vegetable oil
1½ cups sugar
2 eggs
1 teaspoon vanilla
¼ cup milk
½ cup poppy seeds
4 cups flour
2 teaspoons baking powder

Combine oil and sugar. Add eggs, vanilla, and milk. Mix. Add poppy seeds. Blend in flour and baking powder and mix lightly until smooth. Do not overwork dough. Roll out dough to ½-inch thickness and cut out with cookie cutters. Bake on ungreased cookie sheet for 12 minutes.

YIELD: 4 DOZEN

Springerle

- 1 pound powdered sugar
- 4 egg yolks, well beaten
- 1 tablespoon anise seeds
- Zest from one lemon
- Juice from ½ lemon
- 4 egg whites
- 4 cups flour
- 1½ teaspoons baking powder
- ⅛ teaspoon salt

Blend together powdered sugar and well-beaten egg yolks. Add anise seeds, lemon zest, and lemon juice. Beat egg whites until stiff. Combine flour, baking powder, and salt. Add egg whites and flour mixture alternately to sugar mixture, beating well after each addition. The dough will become very thick and difficult to handle. Roll out on well-floured board to ½-inch thickness. Sprinkle with flour and roll with springerle rolling pin. Cut as many cookies as possible without rerolling. Lay cookies on clean cloth and cover. The next day, brush off excess flour and bake on lightly greased pans at 350 degrees for 10 to 12 minutes. The squares will puff and have imprint of the mold. Store in airtight container.

Yield: 4 dozen

Cheese Wafers

- 2 cups finely grated sharp cheddar cheese
- ¼ cup softened butter
- 1 cup flour
- ½ teaspoon salt
- ¼ teaspoon cayenne pepper
- ½ cup finely chopped walnuts

Combine cheese and butter. Add flour, salt, and cayenne pepper. Fold in nuts. Form dough into a couple of logs and refrigerate for 2 hours. Slice and bake on greased cookie sheet at 350 degrees just until light brown.

YIELD: 1 TO 2 DOZEN

Sweet Tip:

Baking times vary widely depending on your oven. Experiment by first baking one cookie as a test.

Candy Cane Cookies

- 1 cup shortening
- 1 cup powdered sugar
- 1 egg
- 1½ teaspoons almond extract
- 1 teaspoon vanilla
- 2½ cups flour
- 1 teaspoon salt
- ¼ teaspoon baking soda
- Red food coloring
- Peppermint candy canes, crushed
- Sugar

Mix first five ingredients thoroughly. Add flour, salt, and baking soda. Divide dough in half and blend red food coloring into one of the halves. Roll out each half separately and cut into 4-inch strips. For each cookie, twist strips together (candy cane–style) and shape like a candy cane. Bake at 350 degrees for about 10 minutes. Remove, and while still hot, sprinkle with mixture of crushed peppermint candy canes and sugar.

YIELD: 2 TO 3 DOZEN

Old-Fashioned Gingersnaps

2 cups dark molasses
½ cup brown sugar
½ cup water
1 cup shortening
2 teaspoons ground ginger
6½ cups flour
2 teaspoons baking soda
½ teaspoon salt

Cook first three ingredients in saucepan on low heat for 15 minutes. Remove from heat and add shortening and ginger. Set aside until cool. Then add flour, baking soda, and salt. Mix well. Dough should be very stiff. Refrigerate for 2 hours. Roll out as thin as possible on floured board. Cut into small circles and bake on greased cookie sheet at 375 degrees just until slightly brown.

YIELD: 7 DOZEN

Maple Syrup Cookies

¼ cup shortening
¼ cup butter
1 cup sugar
1 cup maple syrup
1 cup sour cream
2 eggs, well beaten
1 teaspoon vanilla
3 cups flour
½ teaspoon salt
1 teaspoon baking soda

Cream together shortening, butter, and sugar. Add maple syrup and sour cream. Blend together eggs and vanilla, and stir into creamed mixture alternately with combined dry ingredients. Don't overwork dough. Chill for 2 hours, then roll out on lightly floured board to ⅛-inch thickness. Bake at 350 degrees on greased cookie sheet for 8 minutes or until golden brown.

YIELD: 4 DOZEN

Pfeffernusse

½ cup shortening
1 cup sugar
1 cup cream
1 teaspoon peppermint extract
5½ cups flour
2 teaspoons baking powder
½ teaspoon salt
1 cup milk

Cream together shortening and sugar. Add cream and extract and beat until fluffy. Combine dry ingredients and add alternately with milk. Work gently until soft dough is formed. Divide dough into 4 parts and chill for 1 hour. Working with one part of the dough at a time, roll out on floured board and cut into long strips. Cut across strips to form small square cookies. Bake on greased cookie sheet at 425 degrees until golden brown.

YIELD: 8 TO 10 DOZEN

Rising agents are of key importance when baking. Don't use old baking powder or soda. If the expiration date has come and gone, throw it out and buy fresh.

Rosemary Crescents

- ½ cup shortening
- 1 cup sugar
- 1 egg
- 5 cups flour
- 1 teaspoon baking powder
- 1 teaspoon baking soda
- ½ teaspoon salt
- 1 teaspoon dried rosemary (finely ground)
- 1 cup buttermilk
- Powdered sugar

Cream together shortening, sugar, and egg. Combine flour, baking powder, soda, salt, and rosemary and add to creamed mixture alternately with buttermilk. Chill dough for 2 hours. Roll out to ½-inch thickness on floured board and cut into circles with cookie cutter. Halve each cookie and gently shape into a crescent. Bake on greased cookie sheet at 350 degrees for 10 minutes. While cookies are still warm, dust very lightly with powdered sugar.

YIELD: 6 DOZEN

Shortbread

- 1 cup shortening
- ½ cup sugar
- ½ cup brown sugar
- 3 egg yolks
- ¼ cup milk
- 2 teaspoons vanilla
- 2¾ cups flour
- 2 teaspoons cream of tartar
- 1 teaspoon baking soda
- ½ teaspoon salt

Cream together shortening, sugars, and egg yolks. Add milk and vanilla. Combine dry ingredients and stir into creamed mixture. Chill 1 hour. Roll out to ½-inch thickness on floured board. Cut into long strips, and then cut again across the strips to form 2-inch squares. Bake on ungreased cookie sheet at 350 degrees for 10 to 12 minutes.

YIELD: 3 DOZEN

Grapefruit Sugar Cookies

½ cup shortening
½ cup butter
1 cup sugar
2 eggs
2½ cups flour
2 teaspoons baking powder
½ teaspoon salt
¾ cup finely chopped
candied grapefruit peel

Cream together shortening, butter, sugar, and eggs. Combine dry ingredients and grapefruit peel and add to creamed mixture. Roll dough to ¼-inch thickness on floured board. Cut into squares or circles. Bake on greased cookie sheet at 350 degrees for 10 minutes.

YIELD: 3 DOZEN

Sweet Tip:

Only use bright, shiny aluminum for cookie baking. Once a sheet is discolored and dark, it tends to overbake or even burn cookie bottoms. Always clean your baking sheets of all oily residue after each baking session.

Creamy Yogurt Cookies

½ cup butter
1 cup sugar
1 well-beaten egg
1 (3 ounce) package cream cheese
3 tablespoons plain or flavored yogurt
1 teaspoon vanilla
2 cups flour
½ teaspoon baking soda
½ teaspoon baking powder
¼ teaspoon salt
Plain or colored sugars

Cream together butter, sugar, and egg. Add softened cream cheese, yogurt, and vanilla. Combine dry ingredients, except sugars, and add to creamed mixture. Chill well. Roll out and cut into circles. Sprinkle with plain or colored sugars and bake at 350 degrees for about 12 minutes.

Yield: 3 dozen

Cinnamon Nut Cookies

1 cup shortening
4 eggs
1 cup sugar
1 teaspoon vanilla
4 cups flour
1 teaspoon baking powder
½ teaspoon salt
1 cup chopped pecans
Cinnamon sugar
Cinnamon cookie decoration candies

Cream together shortening, eggs, sugar, and vanilla. Combine flour, baking powder, and salt. Blend with creamed mixture. Add nuts. Chill in refrigerator for several hours. Form dough into 2 or 3 long rolls and bake on greased cookie sheet at 350 degrees for about 30 minutes. While rolls are still warm, slice into ½-inch slices. Place on cookie sheet and sprinkle with cinnamon sugar. Place a cinnamon candy in center of each cookie and bake another 10 minutes.

Yield: 3 to 4 dozen

Stained Glass Cookies

¾ cup shortening
¾ cup sugar
2 eggs
½ cup milk
1 tablespoon almond extract
4 cups flour
2 teaspoons baking powder
½ teaspoon salt
Butter
Marmalade
Cinnamon
Dried cranberries
Chopped toasted almonds

Cream together shortening, sugar, eggs, milk, and extract. Combine dry ingredients and stir into creamed mixture. Blend well, but don't overwork. Chill dough for 1 hour, then divide into three parts. Roll each part out to ¼-inch thickness on floured board. Spread with scant layer of butter and then marmalade. Sprinkle with cinnamon, dried cranberries, and nuts. Roll tightly into jelly roll. Slice into ½-inch slices and bake on greased cookie sheet at 350 degrees for about 10 minutes.

YIELD: 3 TO 4 DOZEN

Yuletide Crescent Cookies

1 pound butter (4 sticks), softened but not melted
16 ounces cream cheese
4 cups flour
½ teaspoon vanilla
¼ teaspoon salt
Powdered sugar

Filling

1 egg
2 cups chopped walnuts or pecans
¼ cup sugar
1 teaspoon vanilla
Dash salt
Powdered sugar

Cream together first five ingredients and refrigerate 2 hours. Roll out well-chilled dough to ⅛-inch thickness on board coated with powdered sugar. Cut into 2-inch squares and place on greased baking sheet. To make filling, beat egg until frothy. Add next four ingredients and put dollop of filling in center of each dough square. Roll from one corner to its opposite, then bend the dough to form crescent. Roll each cookie slightly in powdered sugar and bake at 350 degrees for 10 to 12 minutes.

Yield: 3 dozen

Mint Slices

1 cup sugar
⅔ cup butter
1 egg
1 teaspoon vanilla
3 drops mint extract
1½ cups flour
½ cup cocoa
½ teaspoon salt
½ teaspoon baking soda
1 cup finely chopped nuts

Cream sugar and butter until fluffy. Add egg, vanilla, and extract and beat well. Combine flour with cocoa, salt, and baking soda. Add to creamed mixture. Add nuts. Shape into rolls 1½ inches in diameter. Wrap in wax paper and chill well in refrigerator. When cookies are wanted, slice thin and bake on ungreased cookie sheet at 350 degrees for 8 to 10 minutes.

YIELD: 6 DOZEN

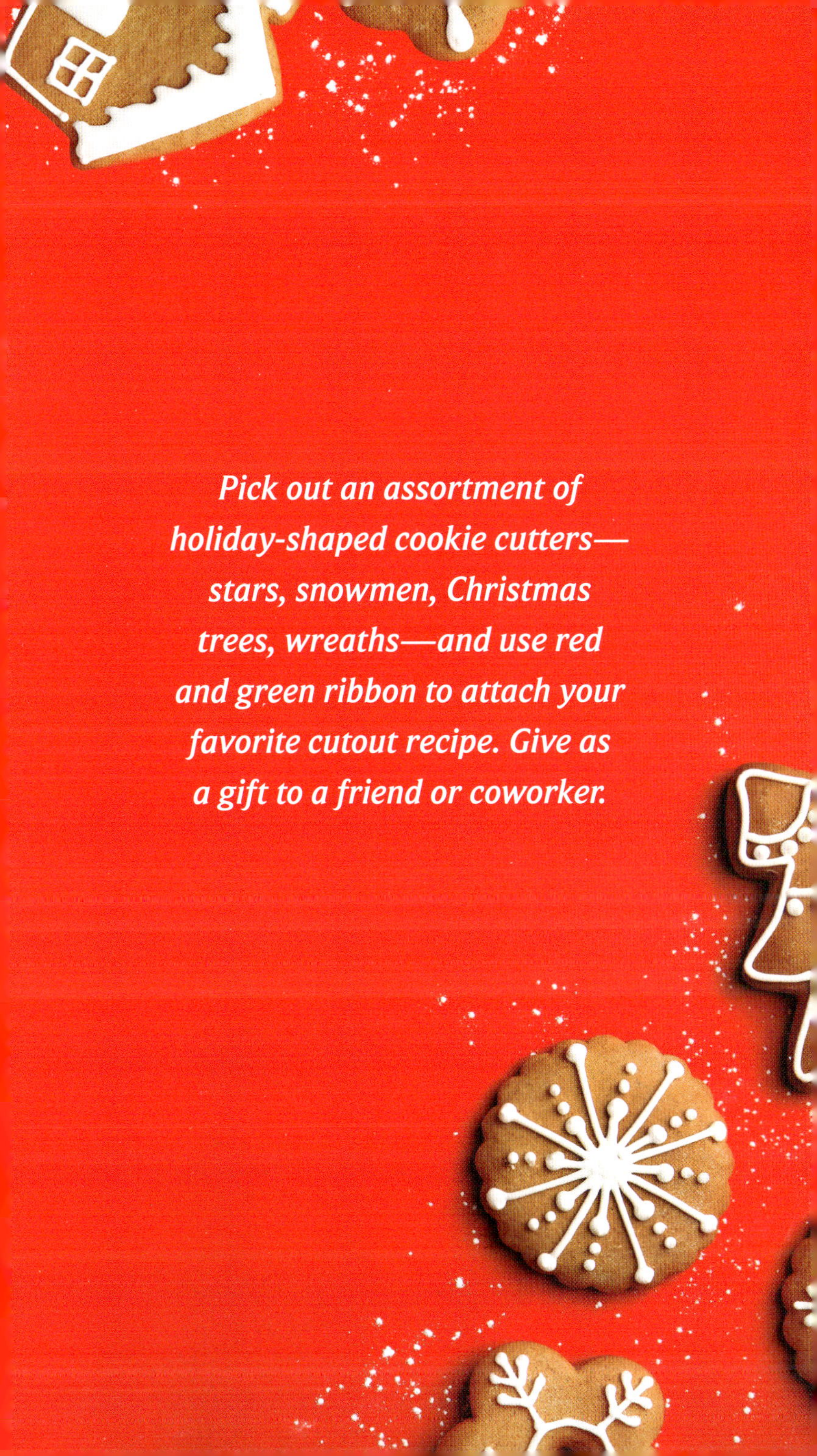

Pick out an assortment of holiday-shaped cookie cutters—stars, snowmen, Christmas trees, wreaths—and use red and green ribbon to attach your favorite cutout recipe. Give as a gift to a friend or coworker.

Filled Cookies

Whether baked and filled, or filled and then baked, this type of cookie has no end of fun, imaginative ingredients. These cookies are a good way to incorporate jams and jellies, creams or ice creams, fluff, custard, candy, or nuts into the most common cookie recipe—and turn it into something spectacular!

Reindeer Pies

- 1 cup shortening
- 2 cups sugar
- 2 eggs
- 1 cup sour milk
- 1 teaspoon lemon juice (optional)
- 1 cup water
- 1 cup instant cocoa mix
- 4 cups flour
- 2 teaspoons soda
- ½ teaspoon salt

Cream together shortening, sugar, and eggs. May add lemon juice to milk to sour it, if needed. Add remaining ingredients and mix well. Drop onto greased cookie sheet and bake at 375 degrees for 8 to 10 minutes. Cool well and sandwich cookies together with frosting of your choice as filling (see frosting recipes starting on page 147).

YIELD: 2 DOZEN

Festive Date-Filled Cookies

1 cup shortening
2 cups brown sugar
3 eggs
½ cup water
1 teaspoon vanilla
3½ cups flour
½ teaspoon salt
1 teaspoon soda
2 dashes cinnamon

FILLING

2 cups chopped dates
¾ cup sugar
¾ cup water
½ cup chopped nuts

Cook filling until thick and add chopped nuts. Cream shortening, brown sugar, eggs, water, and vanilla. Add dry ingredients and mix well. Drop by spoonfuls onto lightly greased cookie sheet. Put ½ teaspoon filling on top of each cookie. Then put ½ teaspoon batter on top of filling. Bake at 375 degrees for 10 to 12 minutes.

YIELD: 2 DOZEN

Jam Thumbprints

- 1 (8 ounce) package cream cheese
- ¾ cup softened butter
- 1 cup powdered sugar
- 2¼ cups flour
- ½ teaspoon baking soda
- ½ cup chopped pecans
- ½ teaspoon vanilla
- Jam or preserves

Beat cream cheese, butter, and powdered sugar until smooth. Add flour and baking soda; mix well. Add pecans and vanilla. Chill dough for about 30 minutes. Shape dough into 1-inch balls and place on ungreased cookie sheet. Press thumb in middle of each cookie. Fill with about 1 teaspoon of your favorite jam or fruit preserves. Bake in 350 degree oven for 14 to 16 minutes.

YIELD: 3 DOZEN

Santa's Favorite Ice-Cream Sandwiches

1 cup shortening
¾ cup sugar
¾ cup brown sugar
1 teaspoon vanilla
2 eggs
2 cups flour
½ teaspoon baking soda
½ teaspoon salt
1 (12 ounce) package semisweet chocolate chips
Granulated sugar
Ice cream, any flavor

Cream together shortening, sugars, vanilla, and eggs. Add dry ingredients and mix well. Stir in chocolate chips. Form dough into large 2-inch balls and space generously on lightly greased cookie sheet. Press each ball down slightly with a glass bottom dipped in granulated sugar. Bake at 325 degrees for 13 to 16 minutes or until slightly brown. When well cooled, sandwich a dollop of your favorite ice cream (just soft enough to spoon) between cookies and press together until well joined and ice cream oozes just to the cookies' edges. Freeze unstacked in individual ziplock bags.

YIELD: 1 DOZEN

Chocolate Whoopie Pies

1½ cups butter or margarine
3 cups sugar
3 eggs
2 teaspoons vanilla
5½ cups flour
⅔ cup cocoa
1½ teaspoons baking soda
1 teaspoon salt
2¼ cups buttermilk

FILLING
Marshmallow fluff
Green or red food coloring

Cream butter and sugar. Add eggs and vanilla and beat until fluffy. Add blended dry ingredients alternately with buttermilk. Chill dough 1 hour. Drop onto greased cookie sheet and bake at 350 degrees for 8 minutes. Let cool. Mix marshmallow fluff with green or red food coloring and spread between cookies.

YIELD: 2 DOZEN

Jam-Filled Sugar Tarts

1 cup sugar
½ cup softened butter
½ cup shortening
3 tablespoons milk
½ teaspoon vanilla
1 egg
3 cups flour
1½ teaspoons baking powder
¼ teaspoon salt
Favorite jam
Granulated sugar

Cream together sugar, butter, shortening, milk, vanilla, and egg. Combine dry ingredients and blend into creamed mixture. Chill dough for 2 hours. Roll out to ¼-inch thickness on floured board. Cut rounds with 2½-inch cutter. Place half the rounds on ungreased cookie sheet. Put dollop of jam in center of each. Top with another round and crimp edges. Sprinkle lightly with granulated sugar. Bake at 375 degrees for 8 to 10 minutes. Remove from cookie sheet immediately after baking.

YIELD: 2 DOZEN

Italian Christmas Cookies

½ cup butter
½ cup shortening
1 cup sugar
1 teaspoon vanilla
5 eggs
5 cups flour
3 teaspoons baking powder
½ teaspoon salt
1 cup sweetened applesauce or apple butter
½ cup crushed walnuts
Granulated sugar
1 cup semisweet chocolate chips
1 tablespoon butter

Cream together ½ cup butter, shortening, sugar, vanilla, and eggs. Combine flour, baking powder, and salt. Add to creamed mixture and mix well. Chill. Roll out to ¼-inch thickness on floured board and cut into 3-inch squares. Fill with mixture of sweetened applesauce or apple butter and crushed walnuts. Fold diagonally to form a triangle. Crimp edges and sprinkle lightly with granulated sugar. Bake at 375 degrees for about 10 minutes. When cool, melt semisweet chocolate chips with 1 tablespoon butter. Dip half of each triangle in chocolate and let set on wax paper.

YIELD: 2 DOZEN

Pineapple-Filled Cookies

¾ cup shortening
1 cup sugar
⅔ cup milk
1 teaspoon vanilla
2 eggs, beaten
4 cups flour
2 teaspoons baking powder
½ teaspoon salt

Filling

1 cup crushed pineapple
½ cup pineapple juice
2 tablespoons lemon juice
2 tablespoons butter
⅔ cup sugar
2 tablespoons flour
¼ teaspoon nutmeg
Dash salt

Prepare filling by combining ingredients in a saucepan at medium heat, stirring constantly until thick and bubbly. Cream together shortening, sugar, milk, vanilla, and eggs. Combine dry ingredients and add to creamed mixture. Blend well. Chill in refrigerator for 1 hour. Roll out to ⅛-inch thickness on floured board. Cut out rounds of 2 inches and place half of them on greased cookie sheet. Place a dollop of filling in the center of each cookie, and then top with another cookie, crimping the edges with a fork. Bake at 350 degrees for 10 minutes.

Yield: 2 dozen

Fig Dainties

1 stick butter
1 cup sugar
2 eggs
3½ cups flour
1 teaspoon baking soda
½ teaspoon salt
½ cup sour milk
1 teaspoon lemon juice (optional)
1 teaspoon vanilla

FILLING

1½ cups chopped figs
¾ cup sugar
2 tablespoons flour
1 cup water
½ cup chopped nuts

Combine all filling ingredients in heavy saucepan. Cook until thick and smooth, stirring constantly. Set aside to cool while preparing dough. Cream together butter, sugar, and eggs. Combine dry ingredients and add alternately with milk (lemon juice may be added to sour the milk) to creamed mixture. Stir in vanilla. Roll out to ¼-inch thickness on floured board. Cut with 3-inch round cookie cutter and place on greased cookie sheet, 2 inches apart. Put 1 teaspoon of filling on each cookie and cover with another cookie, crimping edges securely. Bake at 350 degrees for 10 to 12 minutes.

YIELD: 2 TO 3 DOZEN

Apricot Tart Cookies

½ cup butter

½ cup grated sharp cheddar cheese

1¼ cups flour

FILLING

1 cup dried chopped apricots

⅛ cup water

1 cup sugar

Cream together butter and cheese. Add flour and mix well. Chill for 3 hours. Cook apricots in water for about 10 minutes. Drain and add sugar. Cook and stir for 1 minute. Set aside to cool. Roll dough to ¼-inch thickness. Cut into 2½-inch squares. Place 1 teaspoon of apricot filling on each square and fold diagonally. Crimp edges to seal. Bake on ungreased cookie sheet at 350 degrees for 10 to 12 minutes.

YIELD: 2 TO 3 DOZEN

Chocolate Caramel Cookies

2 sticks butter, softened
¾ cup sugar
¾ cup brown sugar
2 eggs
1 teaspoon vanilla
2 cups flour
½ cup cocoa
1 teaspoon baking soda
½ teaspoon salt
1 cup chopped pecans, divided
1 tablespoon sugar
Large bag chewy chocolate coated caramels
Butter

Cream together butter, sugars, eggs, and vanilla. Combine flour, cocoa, baking soda, and salt. Blend into creamed mixture. Add half of pecans. Chill dough for 2 hours. Add 1 tablespoon of sugar to remaining half the pecans and set aside. Form chilled dough into balls and press dough gently around a caramel to encase it. Brush top lightly with butter and dip top side only in pecan/sugar mixture. Bake on ungreased cookie sheets at 350 degrees for about 10 minutes.

YIELD: 2 TO 3 DOZEN

Apricot Walnut-Filled Cookies

2 sticks butter, softened
2 cups flour
½ teaspoon salt
1 cup cream cheese, softened
1 egg, beaten
1 jar apricot preserves
½ cup walnuts, finely ground

Combine butter, flour, and salt. Work it into crumbles as you would with pastry. Add cream cheese and egg. Chill dough for several hours. Roll to ⅛-inch thick circle on floured board. Spread with light coating of jam and nuts. Cut into thin wedges like a pizza. Starting at wide end, roll each wedge tightly. Bend into a crescent and place seam side down on lightly greased baking pan. Bake at 350 degrees for about 15 minutes.

YIELD: 2 DOZEN

Andes Mint Cookies

1 cup sugar
½ cup brown sugar
½ cup shortening
¼ cup butter
2 eggs
1 teaspoon vanilla
2 tablespoons water
3 cups flour
¾ teaspoon baking soda
½ teaspoon salt
1 package Andes mints
1 egg white
Granulated sugar

Cream together sugars, shortening, butter, eggs, vanilla, and water. Combine dry ingredients and blend into creamed mixture. Chill dough for several hours. Wrap mints individually in well-chilled cookie dough. Space cookies on greased baking sheet so they won't touch while baking. Brush each cookie lightly with egg white that has been beaten to foam. Sprinkle very lightly with granulated sugar. Bake at 350 degrees for 8 to 10 minutes. Watch carefully so cookies don't get too brown.

YIELD: 2 TO 3 DOZEN

Sweet Tip:

When a recipe calls for "softened butter," avoid letting it become runny or melted (unless otherwise directed in the recipe). Oversoftening can leave your dough too thin, and your cookies will spread too much while they bake. Room temperature butter is as soft as it needs to be for most recipes.

Baked goods make wonderful Christmas gifts! Present them in a pretty little basket or decorator box. These can be found at outlets and chain overstock stores for very little cost. Use Christmas tissue paper as a lining, or if you can spend slightly more, line the basket with a bright holiday kitchen towel or table runner, a new set of oven mitts, or a package of paper holiday napkins.

Frosting

Sweet Tip:

When freezing cookies that have been frosted, place them in a single layer on a baking sheet in the freezer for 2 hours. When frozen, they can be stacked or bagged in a freezer container. When ready to use, be sure to separate the cookies in a single layer on a serving tray before they begin to thaw.

Buttercream Frosting

2 cups powdered sugar
½ cup real butter, softened
½ teaspoon salt
1 teaspoon vanilla
Milk

Combine all ingredients except milk. Add milk 2 tablespoons at a time until frosting is the consistency you require.

Variations

For Orange Buttercream:
Replace milk with orange juice.

For Mocha Buttercream:
Add ¼ cup cocoa and 1 teaspoon instant coffee.

Chocolate Buttercream Frosting

2 cups powdered sugar
½ cup cocoa
1 cup butter
½ teaspoon vanilla
½ teaspoon salt
Milk

Combine all ingredients except milk and add 2 tablespoons milk at a time until desired consistency is reached.

Sweet Tip:

Use a stencil or lacy paper to decorate cookies with ease. Place a stencil on top of your cooled cookies, then sift sprinkles, powdered sugar, or cocoa over top. Pull the stencil away, and you'll be left with a fantastic design!

7-Minute Frosting

- 1 cup granulated sugar
- ⅓ cup water
- ½ teaspoon cream of tartar
- ¼ teaspoon salt
- 2 egg whites
- 1 teaspoon vanilla

Mix first four ingredients together in saucepan and boil until sugar dissolves. Add to unbeaten egg whites and beat with electric mixer until stiff, about 7 minutes. Stir in vanilla.

Cream Cheese Frosting

1 package (3 ounces) softened cream cheese
½ cup butter
2 cups powdered sugar
1 teaspoon vanilla
Dash salt
Milk

Combine all ingredients except milk and add milk 2 tablespoons at a time until frosting is desired consistency. For chocolate frosting, add ½ teaspoon cocoa and increase butter by 3 tablespoons.

Caramel Frosting

20 caramels
⅓ cup water
3 tablespoons butter
½ teaspoon salt
2 cups powdered sugar
Chopped walnuts (optional)

Melt caramels in saucepan with water. When smooth, stir in butter and salt. Add sugar until desired consistency is reached. Add walnuts.

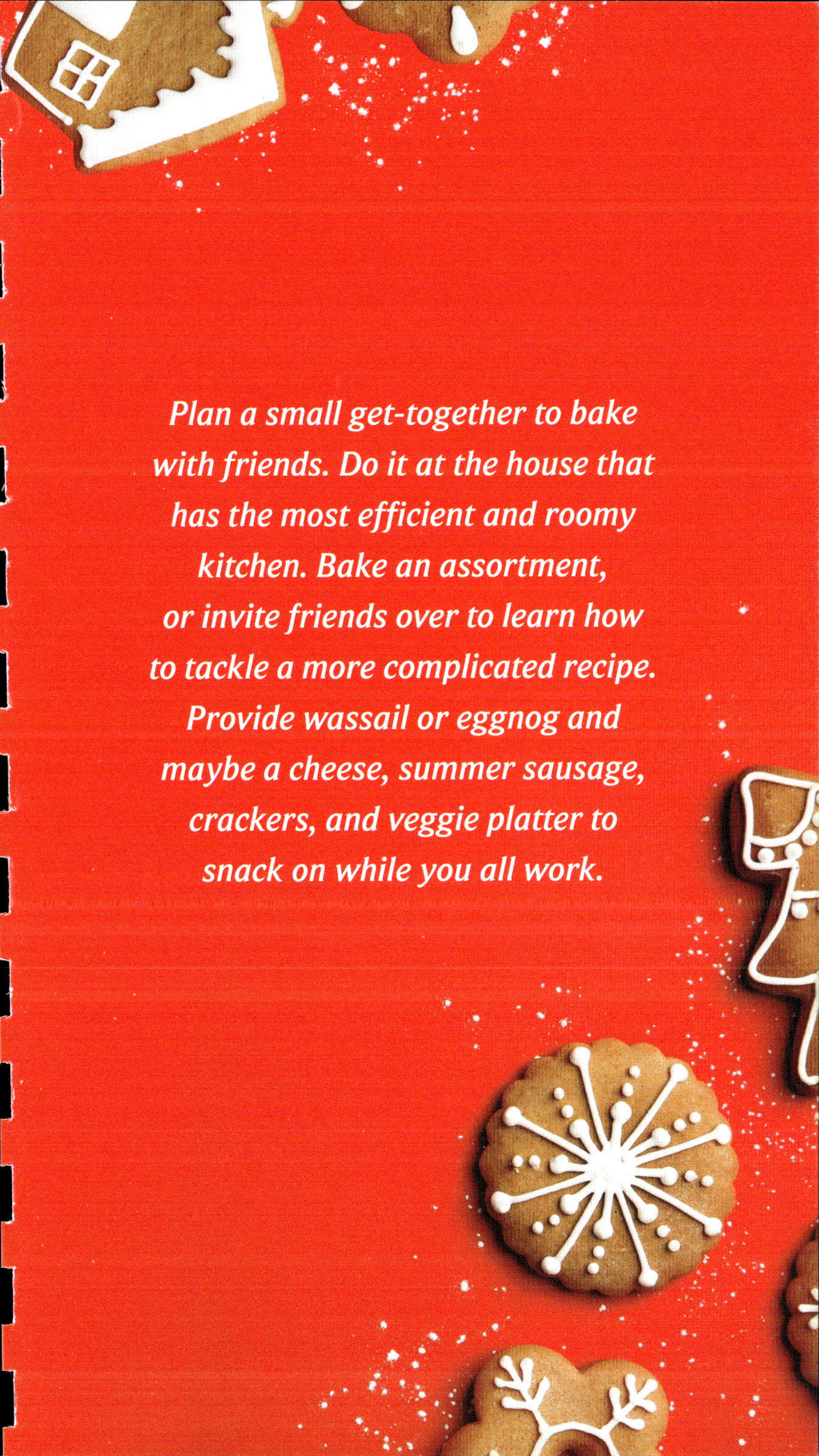

Plan a small get-together to bake with friends. Do it at the house that has the most efficient and roomy kitchen. Bake an assortment, or invite friends over to learn how to tackle a more complicated recipe. Provide wassail or eggnog and maybe a cheese, summer sausage, crackers, and veggie platter to snack on while you all work.

Index

Drop Cookies

Bar Cookies

No-Bake Cookies

Rolled Cookies

Filled Cookies

Frosting